"Death is only an horizon,
only the limit of our sight.

INTRODUCTION

The death of someone close to us can be one of the most painful experiences we will ever suffer. This little book will be a help. It offers reflections on bereavement and the way it affects us. There are prayers too that may be a support and encouragement.

Feel free to use the book in any way you wish. Simply looking at the pictures may be a comfort, or you may want to pause on a line from the Scriptures. We are all different so we react differently, but we can share our feelings and perhaps find assistance to pray.

You may like to read each page in turn, or you may prefer to dip here and there. Use the book in the way that suits you. Skip over parts that do not appeal to you at the moment. Choose what you find helpful.

At the back of the book there are some useful addresses of groups and agencies which are able to offer help.

May God be with you in this time of grief. There is a message of hope when hope seemed gone.

Jesus said, "Know that I am with you
always; yes, to the end of time." (Matthew 28:20)

1

"I am the resurrection and the life. If anyone believes in me, even though he dies he will live, and whoever lives and believes in me will never die." (John 11:25-26)

WHERE THERE IS HOPE

We may feel utterly lost, alone and isolated. We may even feel that God has abandoned us. We have believed in God and now our faith seems empty. We need not fear, for God is with us in our need. We can be one with Christ our Lord as we pray for those we love. Ask the Lord to take care of them. We know that it is in him that we are each to find our peace. And as we pray for the one we love we are confident that he hears our prayer. We discover the unity with Christ that endures all things.

It is no wonder that our Lord says to us, "Do not let your hearts be troubled. Trust in God still, and trust in me". He has prepared a place for us and for those we love. We may feel lost and full of anxiety at the moment when one we love has died. We are bereft and want to know what has happened to them. If we can pause and listen to the voice of God in our hearts we may know that they are at peace.

"But the souls of the virtuous are in the hands of God, no torment shall ever touch them. In the eyes of the unwise, they did appear to die, their going looked like a disaster, their leaving us, like annihilation; but they are in peace." *(Book of Wisdom 3:1-3)*

3

"My help shall come from the Lord
who made heaven and earth...
The Lord will guard you from evil,
he will guard your soul.
The Lord will guard your coming and going
both now and for ever." *(Psalm 121:2,7-8)*

IN THE HANDS OF GOD

All our lives we have known of God's love for us. Now, in our special need, that love is our refuge and strength. Think for a moment of what he has promised to those who love him. The kingdom of heaven is in our midst. Heaven is the fulfilment of all that we have hoped for and longed for: to find love and peace for ever in Christ. This is the secret of happiness. Deep within our hearts we can find that love of God. This is the God who made all things and he shares with us the love that made the world. All the good things we have known are from him. He has waited for us to complete our pilgrimage. We need not fear what he has in store for us. We know he made us for heaven, to enjoy the embrace of our Father in the eternal family of God.

ALONE

We may feel terribly alone, cut off from everybody. We may find it hard to speak. We may feel that no one can understand what we are going through. Yet as we are united with Christ, so we are one in him with the person we love. We can reflect for a moment on these words of prayer: *"May God unite us with all those who have gone before us. May the Lord receive us with his merciful love. May we, redeemed from death, reconciled with our heavenly Father, welcomed by the Good Shepherd, enter fully into the happiness of Christ's eternal kingdom. Amen.*

"At the sight of her tears, and those of the Jews who followed her, Jesus said in great distress, with a sigh that came straight from the heart, 'Where have you put him?' They said, 'Lord, come and see'. Jesus wept; and the Jews said, 'See how much he loved him'." *(John 11:33-36)*

GRIEF

When we suffer a great loss we are certain to be deeply sad. Our sadness may be painful to express. We may want to grieve but feel afraid. We may not want to show our feelings. We may feel we have to be strong for someone else's sake. But this is a time for grief. Jesus wept when his close friend died. And when he saw the grief of the sister of Lazarus he grieved with her.

When we suffer a real loss we may want to cry. It is a natural reaction. This is part of mourning, it is not a weakness or self-indulgence. It is the acknowledgement of loss. We each need to express our sadness in some way and to let those close to us share it with us. They also want to mourn and may need to weep. Each of us mourns in some way when one we love has died.

DIFFERENT REACTIONS

But we each react in different ways. Some become deeply distressed, others distract themselves with details, others again may try to bottle-up their feelings. The sadness has to be expressed in some way. Our grief is very real and it may seem at the moment that it will never end. We may wonder how we can survive the pain of it. We may feel tempted to try to suppress our grief or to fight against it.

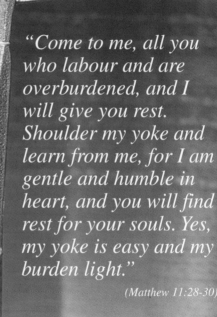

"Come to me, all you who labour and are overburdened, and I will give you rest. Shoulder my yoke and learn from me, for I am gentle and humble in heart, and you will find rest for your souls. Yes, my yoke is easy and my burden light."

(Matthew 11:28-30)

"Do not let your hearts be troubled.
Trust in God still, and trust in me.
There are many rooms in my Father's
  house;
if there were not I should have told you.
I am going now to prepare a place for you,
and after I have gone and prepared you a
  place,
I shall return to take you with me;
so that where I am
you may be too." *(John 14:1-3)*

NUMBNESS

At first we may feel numb. The death of someone close is still a shock to us even if it comes after a long illness. We cannot really take it in. Sometimes we are almost paralysed by it and everything seems unreal and remote. This feeling can last quite a long time. Some find it helpful to be busy involved with the arrangements that have to be made. At the same time it may be that these actions seem far removed from us. We are involved but feel as though everything is at a distance.

ADJUSTING TO THE SHOCK

We may find it difficult to accept that the one we love has died. This is natural. It is nature's way of protecting us from too great a shock. It can be a great help to shield us at first from the full impact of what has happened. But as the truth comes home to us, we may feel a knot of pain inside. Then we begin to express our grief. We may want to sob or to weep. This is good and helps to unravel the pain and tension deep within us.

DEPRESSION

We may begin to feel depressed, anxious, even a bit panicky. Sometimes our depression can have physical effects too. We may suffer sleeplessness or fatigue, our appetite may be affected. We may even feel we are heading for a nervous breakdown. This is all part of our grief.

ANGER

Sometimes grief makes us feel angry – very angry: against God, or the doctors, or even our own family. We may be shocked at our own feelings. But we have no cause to be shocked at ourselves, we have sustained a great blow.

Other members of the family sometimes understand, sometimes they don't. Often they don't know what to do or say. They may share our feelings and be a support to us. But sometimes they will take offence at our anger. We cannot be sure how they will react. Doctors will usually understand. They have met such anger before. But sometimes they also can be upset.

The one person upon whom we can absolutely rely is God. God made us and loves us so he knows what we are going through. He understands our anger. His love will heal the pain. He saw the suffering of his beloved Son on the cross. And Jesus, abandoned by his friends, cried out in agony: "My God, my God, why have you deserted me?" Jesus knows how desolate we can feel.

"But Christ has in fact been raised from the dead, the first-fruits of all who have fallen asleep. Death came through one man and in the same way the resurrection of the dead has come through one man. Just as all men die in Adam, so all men will be brought to life in Christ."
(1 Cor 15:20-22)

GUILT

We can feel guilty for all sorts of reasons. We may wonder whether there was something more we could have done. There are memories that come back to us, memories of things we said and did, memories of opportunities for kindness missed. We want to say sorry and the chance has gone. There are moments we had forgotten until now. If we feel guilt it is part of our grief. Place it in the Lord's hands. He will give us whatever forgiveness we need with his gift of peace.

GRIEF WILL PASS

We may have voiced our anger, so we may voice our pain. The pain also will pass. "Do not be afraid," said Jesus, "Trust in God still, and trust in me." He weeps with us as he wept with Mary and Martha. And gradually, as he shares our suffering, he will help to lift it a little.

"We want you to be quite certain about those who have died, to make sure that you do not grieve about them, like the other people who have no hope. We believe that Jesus died and rose again, and that it will be the same for those who have died in Jesus: God will bring them with him." (1 Thess. 4:13)

HOW LONG WILL OUR GRIEF LAST ?

The suffering may be so great that we are afraid we won't be able to cope. We may be fearful of knowing how long our grief will last. So if we ask "how long?", the answer is as different for each person as each person is different from every other one. Certainly grief can last for a year or even two. Mourning in the heart cannot be hurried or rushed. We will need patience with ourselves and with others around us. We may not want our grief to pass too quickly. But others in their darkest moments may need to know that they will recover. There will be another dawn.

A PRAYER

"May he support us all the day long, till the shadows lengthen and the evening comes, and the busy world is hushed, and the fever of life is over and our work is done. Then in his mercy may he give us a safe lodging and a holy rest and peace at the last."   John Henry Newman

CHILDREN AND DEATH

The child who is bereaved needs also to grieve. Closeness to those they love is important at this time. Children need to share the feelings that we are suffering, otherwise they feel excluded. This can make the child feel guilty. In fact there may already be guilty feelings about thoughtless words or deeds that others have long forgotten. The young person will find it just as hard as everyone else to accept that someone deeply loved has died. The loss is very real and there is need to weep. Tears shared can bring us all closer together.

A LOVED ONE HAS DIED

"We give back to you, O God, those whom you gave to us. You did not lose them when you gave them to us, and we do not lose them by their return to you. Your dear Son has taught us that life is eternal and love cannot die. So death is only an horizon, and an horizon is only the limit of our sight. Open our eyes to see more clearly, and draw us closer to you that we may know that we are nearer to our loved ones, who are with you. You have told us that you are preparing a place for us: prepare us also for that happy place, that where you are we may also be always, O dear Lord of life and death."

"Lead, kindly light, amid th' encircling gloom,
lead thou me on;
the night is dark, and I am far from home,
lead thou me on...
So long thy power hath blest me,
sure it still will lead me on
o'er moor and fen, o'er crag and torrent,
till the night is gone,
and with the morn those angel faces smile
which I have loved long since,
and lost awhile." John Henry Newman

13

OUR HOPE IS IN THE LORD OUR GOD

Out of the depths I cry to you, O Lord,
Lord, hear my voice!
O let your ears be attentive to the voice of my
pleading.
If you, O Lord, should mark our guilt, Lord,
who would survive?
But with you is found forgiveness:
for this we revere you.
My soul is waiting for the Lord,
I count on his word.
My soul is longing for the Lord,
more than watchman for daybreak...
Because with the Lord there is mercy and fullness
of redemption... *(Psalm 130)*

Jesus said, "Yes, it is my Father's will that whoever sees the Son and believes in him shall have eternal life, and that I shall raise him up on the last day."
(John 6:40)

"Near the cross of Jesus stood his mother:.."
(John 19:25)

Mary, the mother of Jesus, suffered the darkness of grief when the dead body of her son was taken down from the cross. In our grief we can take comfort in her sorrow. Her faith was unshaken. We may quietly contemplate the love that God has given us and that can never be taken from us. United with Christ we share a sure sign of hope and comfort.

The Lord's my shepherd, I'll not want,
he makes me down to lie
in pastures green. He leadeth me
the quiet waters by.

My soul he doth restore again,
and me to walk doth make
within the paths of righteousness,
e'en for his own name's sake.

Yea, though I walk in death's dark vale,
yet will I fear none ill.
For thou art with me, and thy rod
and staff me comfort still.

My table thou has furnished
in presence of my foes,
my head thou dost with oil anoint,
and my cup overflows.

Goodness and mercy all my life
shall surely follow me.
And in God's house for evermore
my dwelling-place shall be.

(Paraphrased from Ps 23 in the "Scottish Psalter" 1650)

RESOURCES

Cruse Bereavement Care – offers help to all bereaved people. There are 150 local branches around the country. The headquarters will always help: Cruse House, 126 Sheen Road, Richmond, Surrey, TW9 1UR. (Tel. 020-8939-9530)

Compassionate Friends – this is an international organisation of bereaved parents offering friendship and understanding to other bereaved parents. If you cannot find them locally then contact: Compassionate Friends, 53, North Street, Bristol, BS3 1EN. (Tel. 0117 9539639)

Sands – Stillbirth and Neonatal Death Society helps parents who have experienced stillbirth or neonatal deaths. There are a number of branches around the country. In case of difficulty contact: 28 Portland Place, London W1B 1LY. (Tel. 020-7436-5881)

Help The Aged is an advice service for elderly people, their relatives, friends and carers. They have published a leaflet entitled "Bereavement" with advice about the emotional and practical aspects of dealing with bereavement. Contact: Help the Aged, 207–221 Pentonville Road, London N1 9UZ. (Tel. 020-7278-1114)

Age Concern – a national network of groups providing services for elderly people and their carers. Some Age Concern groups also offer bereavement counselling. To find your local group look up Age Concern in your 'phone book. In case of difficulty contact: **Age Concern England** – Astral House, 1268 London Road, London SW16 4ER (Tel. 020-8765-7200) **Age Concern Scotland** – 113 Rose Street, Edinburgh, EH2 3DT (Tel. 0131 220 3345)

You may also obtain help from:
The Citizens Advice Bureau will have a local branch somewhere near you. They will help with practical problems following a death. They are sure to be a help also with any advice or counselling that is needed.

The Department of Health and Social Security have published two pamphlets that will help:
D49 "What to do after a death" is a comprehensive guide to what you will need to do and the help that is available to you.
NP45 "A widow's guide" offers general guidance for benefits
You can obtain these pamphlets from your local Social Security Office.

Copyright © Redemptorist Publications
A Registered Charity limited by guarantee.
Registered in England 3261721

Text: Michael McGreevy, C.SS.R.
Design: Roger Smith

Photographs: Cover Zefa-Stockmarket
Pages 2 & 3, 5: David Toase
Page 7: Andrew Thomas
Pages 12 & 13: David Alexander

Revised Anglican edition, published September 1994
Eighth Printing March 2003 (43rd thousand)

ISBN 0 85231 147 8

Printed by Lithgo Press Limited LE8 6NU

Redemptorist
PUBLICATIONS
Alphonsus House Chawton Hampshire GU34 3HQ
Telephone 01420 88222   Fax 01420 88805
rp@ShineOnline.net   www.ShineOnline.net